CELIA'S BIRTHDAY

CHELSEA KONG

© 2024-2025 Chelsea Kong

All rights reserved. All images used in this book are licensed copies from their respectful owners including Jasmine Kong, Freepik, Ghetty Images, Canva, others. This book or any portion thereof may not be reproduced or used in any manner whatsoever without the express written permission of the publisher except for the use of brief quotations in a book review.

Printed in 2024-2025, Made in Toronto, Canada
ISBN: 978-1-998335-06-0
Library and Archives Canada

It is finally Celia's birthday!
She got so excited.

Birthdays are a special time of the year.

Most people celebrate it only once a year.

Make your birthday special with some cheer!

What would you wish for now that you know?

Be thankful and joyful every day!

We should never be alone.
And being sad is bad.

One should never lose the good things to come.

Helping others and share.
Always bless others.

There is so much more
for you and me to explore!

Then you will receive
that which your heart desires.

Birthdays open the door for so much more!

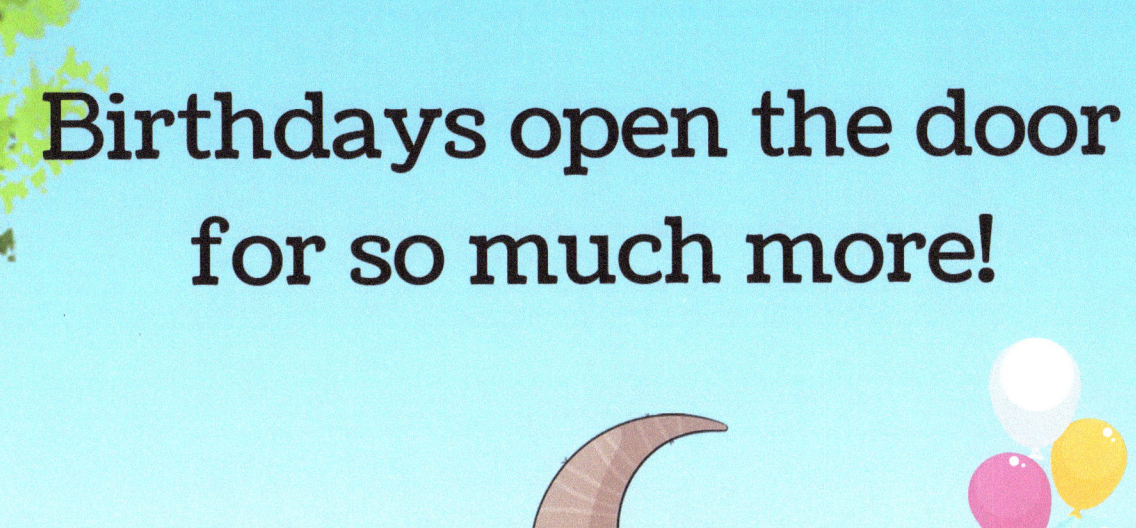

Friends who share will always care for you.

More will come.
That is so much more fun.

Even in the ocean floor.
There is beauty all around.

Hare Facts

LIFE: 4-8 YEARS AND SOMETIMES UP TO 12 YEARS.
SIZE: GROWS UP TO 40-70 CENTIMETRES (2.4 TO 4.3 INCHES).
FOOD: GRASS, FRUITS, VEGETABLES, SEEDS, NUTS, AND SOME FUNGI.

Hare Facts

THEIR SPEED: 70 KILOMETRES OR 43 MILES PER HOUR.
WITH LONGER EARS AND TALLER HIND LEGS, THEY LOOK LARGER RABBITS.
HARES LIVE ABOVE GROUND.

Hare Facts

A BABY RABBIT IS CALLED A BUNNY.
THE MALE RABBIT IS JACK.
THE FEMALE RABBIT IS JILL.

Hare Facts

HARES ARE FOUND IN EURASIA, AFRICA, NORTH AMERICA AND JAPANESE ARCHIPELAGO.

Hare Facts

THEIR HIND LEGS ARE POWERFUL
AND CAN LEAP MORE
THAN 3 METRES OR 10 FEET.
THEY SLEEP IN THE DAYTIME.

Hare Facts

THE SNOWSHOE HARE HAS FUR THAT TURNS WHITE TO HELP THEM HIDE.
IN SPRING, THEIR FUR IS SHORTER AND LOOKS MORE BROWN.
HARES LIKE TO LIVE ALONE AND LIKE TO STAY AWAKE AT NIGHT.

Hare Facts

THEY STAY CLOSE TO THE GROUND AND MAKE THEIR EARS LIE FLAT ON THEIR BACKS

Hare Facts

FEMALE HARES ARE READY TO HAVE BABIES FOR 42 DAYS.
THEY HAVE TO 1-8 BABIES AT A TIME.
EACH YEAR, THEY CAN HAVE THREE LITTERS.

Hare Facts

JACK RABBITS ARE HARES.
THEY ARE BROWN.
YOUNG HARES CALLED LEVERETS CAN HOP A FEW MINUTES AFTER BIRTH.

Rabbit Facts

EAR LENGTH: GROWS UP TO 10 CENTIMETERS AND TURNS 180 DEGREES
THEY HAVE LONG EARS, BIG HIND LEGS, AND SHORT FUR.
FOOD: GRASS, WILDFLOWERS AND VEGETABLES (CARROTS AREN'T THAT GOOD FOR THEM.)

Rabbit Facts

A BABY RABBIT IS CALLED A KIT.
THE MALE IS CALLED A BUCK.
THE FEMALE IS CALLED A DOE.

Rabbit Facts

THEY CAN JUMP HIGH.
THEY HAVE SHARP HEARING.
THEIR TEETH KEEP GROWING.

Rabbit Facts

THEY LIKE TO LIVE IN GROUPS.
THEY LIVE IN WARRENS
(MADE OF MANY TUNNELS
AND ROOMS DUG UNDERGROUND).

Rabbit Facts

MOTHER RABBITS ARE READY
TO HAVE A BABY FROM 28 TO 31 DAYS.
THEY HAVE UP TO 14 BABY RABBITS
AT ONE TIME: CALLED KITTENS

LET'S SEE WHAT YOU REMEMBER BY DOING SOME ACTIVITIES!

Activities

Hare Word Search

Alone
Above
America
Hare

Leap
Longer
Night
Taller

Hare Word Search

C	L	F	Z	R	E	L	L	A	T
Z	K	P	H	T	D	Y	Q	U	D
Q	J	A	B	O	V	E	W	J	C
P	R	E	Q	C	S	J	V	B	X
E	U	L	O	N	G	E	R	P	E
N	C	T	R	F	B	G	E	Q	N
D	O	Y	H	U	M	N	C	S	O
J	L	F	T	G	D	Y	G	H	L
U	M	H	A	C	I	R	E	M	A
V	B	X	F	O	Z	N	H	Z	J

Rabbit Word Search

Buck
Doe
Grass
Hides

Jump
Kit
Rabbit
Tunnels

Rabbit Word Search

R	L	X	K	E	N	L	Y	K	D
F	K	C	Z	C	X	I	B	Q	O
P	U	A	O	B	H	Z	W	J	E
B	T	L	N	T	I	K	C	U	V
C	P	F	Q	O	D	G	V	M	L
N	Y	D	J	F	E	U	A	P	C
D	G	R	A	S	S	N	Q	W	U
Z	L	C	Q	J	P	Y	V	L	T
U	M	T	I	B	B	A	R	D	F
S	L	E	N	N	U	T	H	Z	J

Hare Crossword

Across

2. They know how to _____ on trees.

5. They eat bamboo _____ and shoots.

Down

1. Red Pandas can be found in a place that begins with M.

3. They are like weasels, skunks, and this animal.

4. They live in in a place that begins with N.

6 They _____ their fur like cats.

7. They like to climb on _____.

Hare Crossword

Rabbit Crossword

Across

1. Hare is _____ than rabbits.

4. They like to live _____.

7. They love to ____ high.

Down

2. The like to live _____ ground.

3. There ears are _____ than rabbits.

4. You can find them in a place the starts with A.

6 The opposite of day.

8. A baby Jack and Jill belongs to a _____.

Rabbit Crossword

Hare Scrambled
Unscramble to get the answer.

Earh

Vobea

Noeal

Ceraiam

Grearl

Lleart

Ongl

Htign

Rabbit Scrambled
Unscramble to get the answer.

Briatb

Oed

Mpuj

Teeth

Itk

Esnunlt

Kcub

Usogpsr

LET'S SEE HOW YOU DID!

Answers

Hare Word Search

C	L	F	Z	R	E	L	L	A	T
Z	K	P	H	T	D	Y	Q	U	D
Q	J	A	B	O	V	E	W	J	C
P	R	E	Q	C	S	J	V	B	X
E	U	L	O	N	G	E	R	P	E
N	C	T	R	F	B	G	E	Q	N
D	O	Y	H	U	M	N	C	S	O
J	L	F	T	G	D	Y	G	H	L
U	M	H	A	C	I	R	E	M	A
V	B	X	F	O	Z	N	H	Z	J

Rabbit Word Search

R	L	X	K	E	N	L	Y	K	D
F	K	C	Z	C	X	I	B	Q	O
P	U	A	O	B	H	Z	W	J	E
B	T	L	N	T	I	K	C	U	V
C	P	F	Q	O	D	G	V	M	L
N	Y	D	J	F	E	U	A	P	C
D	G	R	A	S	S	N	Q	W	U
Z	L	C	Q	J	P	Y	V	L	T
U	M	T	I	B	B	A	R	D	F
S	L	E	N	N	U	T	H	Z	J

Hare Crossword

Rabbit Crossword

Hare Scrambled
Unscramble to get the answer.

Hare   Above

Alone   America

Larger   Taller

Long   Night

Rabbit Scrambled
Unscramble to get the answer.

Rabbit   **Doe**

Jump   **Teeth**

Kit   **Tunnels**

Buck   **Groups**

References

National Geographic Kids, "10 Hopping Fun Rabbit Facts." National Geographic Kids, 2015-2024
https://journeynorth.org/tm/eagle/Facts_Ecology.html

Tons of Facts, "27 Fun and Interesting Facts about Hares." 2020 Tons of Facts
http://tonsoffacts.com/27-fun-interesting-facts-hares/

Britannica, "Hare." Animals & Nature
https://www.britannica.com/animal/hare-mammal

Thank you for reading this book. I hope you can leave a good review to encourage me to write more books to teach children and adults. Celia's Birthday is fun to write, and I wanted a book that also talks about how important it is to celebrate your birthday. In my faith, we believe it opens the doors of blessings and opportunities more than other times of the year. This is when Christians should ask God to grant them everything that is right in His eyes that we want.

OTHER PRODUCTS

- Knowing God
- How to Hear God's Voice
- New Life in Jesus
- Loving Israel
- God's Gifts/Spiritual Talents
- Meeting God
- Word Power
- Fruit of the Spirit
- The Tabernacle
- Bride for Jesus
- A Life of Prayer
- Live Free
- Who am I in Jesus
- Walk in Love
- God's Favor
- Man of God
- Woman of God
- How to Use Money
- God's Wisdom
- Fasting
- See Jerusalem and Bethany
- First Fruit Offering
- Feast of Trumpets
- Day of Atonement
- Feast of Tabernacles
- Counting the Omer
- Festival of Lights
- Glory, Presence, and Holy Spirit
- Live in God's Presence
- Pentecost
- See Galilee, Nazareth, and Tiberias
- Hear God Speak
- Knowing Jesus
- Knowing Holy Spirit
- A Healthy Life and Healthy Life Work Book
- Smokey the Cat
- Passover Unleavened Bread
- Resurrection Life
- The Blessing
- Revival
- Chelsea Learns Hebrew
- Thanksgiving
- Give Thanks
- Jesus Birth
- Loving Jesus: Bride and Groom
- Proverbs 31 Woman

OTHER PRODUCTS

ABC of People in the Bible
Colours in the Bible
Breakthroughs
Open Doors
The Seven Spirits of God
Numbers in the Bible
Aglee the Eagle
An Eagle's Life
Chelsea Learns Numbers in Hebrew
ABC's of Faith
Feast of Purim
A Royal Life
Pandas
Worship

Devotionals
31 Day Devotional

Inspirational/Other
Chelsea's Psalms and Poems
Your Daily Meal: Chelsea's Photo Album
Chelsea's Psalms and Poems2
Travel West Caribbean

Puzzle Books
Biblical Puzzle Book Vol 1-5
Bible Puzzles for Young Children Book 1-3
Biblical Puzzle for Children Books 1-5

OTHER PRODUCTS

Teaching Series

How to Hear God's Voice Teaching Guide & Audio Book
Relationship with God, Jesus, Holy Spirit Guide
Knowing God, Jesus, Holy Spirit Guide & Audio Book
Flowing in the Prophetic

Teaching (Non-Sale on my website)
Purim
Passover
Resurrection

BOOK REVIEWS

More books on Amazon, Kobo, and Barnes and Noble, Smashwords, and IngramSpark.
https://chelseak532002550.wordpress.com/

More books on Amazon, Kobo, and Barnes and Noble, Smashwords, and IngramSpark.
https://www.amazon.com/author/chelseakong

Please leave a review and share with friends to help the author continue to write more books to reach more readers. Thank you so much for your support.

Review!

About
CHELSEA KONG

She is a writer, creative arts and digital media artist, skilled administration and payroll professional, and podcaster. Chelsea also served in a variety of roles, from audiovisual, photography, to assisting on the worship team, and ministry team. She also has a passion for families being united.

Chelsea has been a guest on Unity Live Radio, The Lady Tracey Show, and How to Live for Christ and is highly recommended by a Proud Christian blog. She is also a guest blogger. A few of her books have been featured in YourAuthorHub, etc. She graduated from Hotel and Restaurant Management, Digital Media Arts, Office Administration, Payroll Professional, and experience working with children. Chelsea lives in Toronto, Canada. She mainly writes children's books, stories, bridal writing, poems, lyrics for songs, words of encouragement, blessings, prayers, and jokes. The author of How to Hear the Voice of God, the Bridal Collection, Knowing God, etc. She also has her own Bible Puzzle books and other inspired products. Her podcast channel is called Chelsea K on Anchor, Spotify, and iTunes.

Please check my website to find out more:
https://chelseak532002550.wordpress.com/

www.ingramcontent.com/pod-product-compliance
Lightning Source LLC
Chambersburg PA
CBHW042006150426
43194CB00003B/144